The bumper cars

By Beverley Randell
Illustrated by Elspeth Lacey

"Come here, Dad,"
said James.
"Look at the bumper cars."

Dad and James
looked at the bumper cars.

Nick and Kate
looked at the cars, too.

"Dad, can I go in a car?"
said James.
"Can I go in the red car?"

Kate said,
"Can I go, too?"

Kate and James are in the red car.

Nick said,
"Here is a blue car.
Come on, Dad.
Can we go
in the blue car?"

"Look, Dad!
Here comes the red car,"
shouted Nick.
"Here comes Kate!"

"Here we come!"
shouted Kate.
"**Here we come!**"